Me and My Friends

I Can Be a Friend

written by Daniel Nunn

illustrated by Clare Elsom

Heinemann
LIBRARY

Chicago, Illinois

© 2015 Heinemann Library,
an imprint of Capstone Global Library, LLC
Chicago, Illinois

All rights reserved. No part of this publication may be reproduced or transmitted in any form or by any means, electronic or mechanical, including photocopying, recording, taping, or any information storage and retrieval system, without permission in writing from the publisher.

Edited by Brynn Baker
Designed by Steve Mead and Kyle Grenz
Production by Helen McCreath
Original illustrations © Clare Elsom
Originated by Capstone Global Library Ltd

Library of Congress Cataloging-in-Publication Data
Cataloging-in-publication information is on file with the Library of Congress.

ISBN 978-1-4846-0245-4 (paperback)
ISBN 978-1-4846-0255-3 (ebook PDF)

Contents

Being a Friend 4
Being Friendly Quiz 20
Picture Glossary 22
Index 22
Notes for Teachers
and Parents 23
In this Book. 24

Being a Friend

I **share** with my **friend**.

Good friends share.

I take turns with my friend.

Good friends take turns.

I tell the truth to my friend.

Good friends tell the truth.

I listen to my friend.

Good friends listen.

I **care** for my friend.

Good friends care.

I help my friend.

Good friends help.

I play nicely with my friends.

Good friends play nicely.

I have fun with my friends!

Good friends have fun!

Being Friendly Quiz

Which of these pictures shows being friendly?

Did being friendly make these children happy? Why?
Do you like being friendly?

Picture Glossary

care to watch over your friends with feelings of concern and sympathy

friend person you care about and have fun with

share to divide equally or take turns

Index

caring 12, 13
having fun 18, 19
helping 14, 15
listening 10, 11

playing nicely 16, 17
sharing 4, 5
taking turns 6, 7
telling the truth 8, 9

Notes for Teachers and Parents

BEFORE READING

Building background: Ask children to describe what makes a good friend. How do they make friends? What's the best thing about having a friend?

AFTER READING

Recall and reflection: Ask the class how children in the book had fun. What things do they like to do? (playing a game, jumping rope) Do children in the book look happy? How can they tell?

Sentence knowledge: Choose a page, and have children identify a capital letter and a period. Why is there a capital letter? What does a period signal?

Word knowledge (phonics): Have children point to the word *with* on page 4. Sound out the three phonemes in the word *w/i/th*. Ask children to sound out each phoneme as they point at the letters, and then blend the sounds together to make the word *with*. Ask them which of these words have the same sound in the middle, *pin, pan, bit, but, ten,* or *tin*.

Word recognition: Look at the word *nicely* on page 17. Help children to clearly hear the two syllables. (nice/ly) Say the word slowly while clapping once for each syllable.

AFTER-READING ACTIVITIES

Ask children to work with partners to draw a picture of something they like to do with good friends. They can write a sentence or dictate a sentence about the picture. Bind the pages into a class book about friendship.

In this Book

Topic
friendship

Topic Words and Phrases
care
friends
have fun
help
play
share
take turns
tell the truth

Sentence Stems
I ___ for my friend.
I ___ to my friend.
I ___ with my friend.
Good friends ___.

High-frequency Words
for
have
I
my
the
to
with